Mo

Moss on a Rolling Stone

To Mr. Malcolm
&
Mrs. Lynnbeth,
With much
love,
Kelsie Stone

Kelsie Stone
USA

Moss on a Rolling Stone

ISBN-13:
978-1463679200

ISBN-10:
1463679203

Printed in the United States of America.

What a lovely thing a poem can be,
Painting pictures of sadness and love.
Telling of stories and things you'd never see,
Like battles and anguish or a one-winged dove.

Moss on a Rolling Stone

This is for you.

I would like to thank my wonderful parents, for being all they can be and all I've ever needed. You are so supportive and honest about everything.

I'd also like to extend thanks to all my friends from school, those people I've grown up with, those I haven't, for listening to my endless writing in class and refusing to stop praising and encouraging me.

A big thank-you goes to Mrs. CJ as well, for all the support and praise in class.

And thank-you so much to Grandma Dodie and Grandma Irene, for listening to my writing for all these years and all the support and encouragement you've shown me.

Finally, my favorite and only sister. Your blunt, to-the-point criticism is well appreciated. Thanks for being there for me.

Contents

Prejudices can be in the form of jealousies…

Facemask

October 19th, 2010

A different face precedes me,
My colors are not true.
Before you judge me consider,
That I might be the same as you.

Just because I'm confident at school,
Just because my smile's common.
Doesn't mean my heart is happy,
Maybe inside I'm cold and solemn.

Because my life seems perfect,
Because jealousy's directed at me.
It could show my heartfelt neglect,
And all the pain that you can't see.

If one day, you see my tears,
Don't look so surprised.
Everyone needs a friend, you see,
To take off their well-built disguise.

What a war that awaits us…

A Looming Battle

October 20th, 2010

As pain and desire, lift them up,
A cold hand waits, the master of dread.
When darkness conforms to hearts corrupt,
You must be careful, or end up dead.

Blood is gathering, new and old,
Patrons show their children a side.
And forces gather, growing bold,
Good or evil, you must decide.

Before the darkness splits in two,
And evil shows his broken face.
Before the young are death imbued,
We rush to meet a deadly embrace.

Weapons that stood, in dusty solitude,
Awaiting a battle centuries old.
Now gleaming and polished, in silent gratitude,
Their blades are keen, their soldiers bold.

In battle we stand, strong and tall,
Awaiting the soldiers of hell.
As a fight long awaited begins,
Our lovely warriors stood or fell.

A story of suffering, forged into strength

Falling Crystals

October 22nd, 2010

Eyes, they glimmer with unborn words,
They hold back their sorrow as long as they can.
With broken lives, in a broken world,
The crystals that plague them are painfully bland.

A crystal falls, it shatters, liquefied.
The shards of beauty bleed out of the floor.
While shadows dance and sing of lies,
A crystal dies, followed by more,

The crystals fall in silent beauty,
Their ashes are water, their energy sorrow.
With thwarted love and broken souls,
They carry dead hopes with the promise of tomorrow.

What sad choices we have made…

Useless Love

October 27th, 2010

We're caught in this endless, repeating love,
My dreams threaten me with blood.
Through time and space and broken fears,
This moment, this love, we'll never speak of.

Your words caress away my fears,
Your courage guides my fragile heart.
Your love staunches my flow of tears,
A final kiss before we part.

It's useless, my love. Utterly so,
We cannot meet without strife.
Before our dreams are buried below,
I bid you farewell, you're gone from my life.

These tears I cry, above your grave,
Sorrow fills my wounded heart.
Love, my love, don't leave. Please stay.
We kissed, but once. For now we part.

Memories gone.

The Washing Storm

October 27th, 2010

The rain begins to cleanse the Earth,
Our tears are cascading down.
In an abandoned house lies a stone-cold hearth,
Where a rusty fire once was found.

The ghost of the fire flickers slowly,
Its phantom flames attack the skies.
Illuminating foliage dead and molding,
While particles on false thermals rise.

The prison is within you…

Inlaid Dreams

October 29th, 2010

Broken, watching dreams slide by,
Sitting, standing, yet paralyzed.
Unable to grasp the wonder escaping to the skies-
His torture's reason; He wonders, why?

He's eternally watching others dream,
Trying to grasp the happier moments.
Attempting to fend nightmares back to Hades,
But unable to move, crying in loneliness.

His eternal punishment, his forever prison,
Unable to cease the suffering.
But his defiance, like a serpent hissing,
His ability to wake, setting gray worlds coloring.

And so he opens his eyes,
To the dream inlaid with such pain's demise.

Time. A lovely concept.

Rewind

November 10th, 2010

Click. Shuddering movements slow and rewind,
Back before this mistake was made.
Leave this painful past behind,
Before that deadly foundation was laid.

Take back a victim fallen to the knife,
Before that crime was ever committed.
Before she jumped, gave up her life,
Rewind- but what consequences from thought are omitted?

A pressed button, a snap of his fingers,
Time jumps back to obey.
Yet the lover of death, bad-news bringer,
Consequences will abound today.

How could anguish speak through words…?

Despair

November 12th, 2010

Sadness drags my spirit down,
Agony tries my mind.
Coldness seeps into my soul,
And light I cannot find.

And what can lovely despair do?
Entitle you for a broken soul.
Because the blame is cast on you,
Despair claws a gaping wound.

Have you ever stood in the rain… and wondered?

The Sorrow Storm

November 12th, 2010

Run, gallop through the streets,
I'll show you how to fly.
Thunder booms as our hearts beat,
The storm breaks, the sky, it cries.

Faceted tears, the skies' despair,
It streams down in rivulets of pain.
Broken in sorrows ever fair,
The skies gaze down at beauty, in vain.

Hatred lies in a shallow grave…

Lovely Ice

November 15th, 2010

Frozen, chilled in ugly fears,
Colder than the blackest ice.
The heart of a thousand tears,
Sorrow grips it like a vice.

Eternally frozen, dark as night,
Weeping a thousand tears.
Not even scorched by day's first light,
Hot to the touch, human love it sears.

Darker than sorrow by which dreams do die,
Harder than diamonds of useless fortune.
Immortally alone, eternally night,
Imprisoned by the pain it was borne in.

Who is the remedy to death?

A Dying Soul

November 17th, 2010

This broken life,
A sickened soul.
My heart they bind,
And bore a hole.

My tears, oh, none will fall,
My heart, hear me, it will not beat.
A mute bird cannot sing or call,
And on death's door we'll meet.

Believe me when I say I'm sick,
Though tears I do not cry.
The illness is much deeper though,
And so I do not feel or cry.

The illness is down in my soul,
Where dreams are born or die.
Each passing night I feel the cold,
Whilst on Death's door I lie.

Life is more than a visual.

Write

November 20th, 2010

My emotion pours from the tip of my pain,
Turning dark with my malice,
Fading cold with disdain,
Like a seven-sided dice.

I retreat into shadow,
Life is mind full of matter.
My body is left, cold and hollow,
Whilst my mind opposes the latter.

When I think, I think of you…

How Long Have You Been Gone?

December 13th, 2010

I've missed you for a while now,
You haunt my dreams and sleep.
I close my eyes, my head is bowed,
But slumber still I seek.

You see, I lay me down and think,
Of your smile, strong and true.
Your laugh and love, your will-forged link,
To me with all you do.

Sometimes, I admit, I say,
The tears just pour on down.
Like a hurricane on a misty day,
My strength is nowhere found.

And when I cry, what mends the pain?
My broken disposition.
When sorrow fills my bled-out heart,
Who sews closed the heart's incision?

For love has long been a dastardly thing,
A want of pain and strife.
Like endless waves on an endless shore,
Or the glint of a rusty knife.

Sorrow fills my soul today,
But once I glance around.

And when so I have, who do I spy?
For my steady strength is here and found.

And once, when I see your smile,
That cheerful greeting of yours.
You see, it mends my aching heart,
And touches relief where my soul is sore.

You call my name, I look at you,
You haunt my steps in all I do.
The love I feel is caught by pain,
Because our future is sought, in vain.

Like a metaphor to dawn…

Glass Screams

December 20th, 2010

Silence.
The coldness of dead words surrounds me.
Quiet, hush, I can hear your thoughts break.
In the morning, before the shattered sky submits to defeat.
Every star a window to another galaxy,
When daylight comes the glass of those windows breaks in pain,
And we can hear them cry, oh, subject to hear them scream.

Such an ugly truth we are.

Thin Souls

September 27th, 2010

Darkness fills the heart as sins thrive in humanity,
Pain is ever confident when we ignore the present light.
God is reaching out; He loves and sorrows; those less fortunate and me,
While in torture, humanity. Sins and darkness prevail by night.

As sorrow fills the T.V. screen, and blackness cloaks our minds,
Our hearts and souls crave food and drink; we starve them to stay thin.
We numb our minds to relationships and hide behind our screens,
As blood begins to clot the veins of life to which we cling.

Be**lie**ve in lies of those hypocrites whose lips apparently spew truth,
as we nod our heads and make our beds and pretend to understand.
Obediently we repeat their words and take to heart their lack of use,
before trials conform us to their bloody battles and so called holy land.

Beware! They cry. The land you walk upon is thin,
Because no one before you has dared to stand upon it.

And so because we do not understand it, battles we must win,
We must be careful of land we do not belong in.

As shadows twist, contort our vision. Make lies seem to be true,
Who has stood where you do now? Beware knowledge of fear.
Because the darkness killed our souls and resistance is no use,
We might as well go along with them and March like the fools we are.

Absence of light creates a shadow…

Shadowleap

December 23rd, 2010

The shadows leap forward; they're watching the skies,
In cold and in darkness, they sit in disguise.
While waiting for time and night yet to come,
The watchers of darkness, afraid of light's rise.

In fellowship of the shadows,
Whilst the darkened flames do dance.
As the moon begins to rise they fall,
And hide behind this chance.

In spite of their trials, which showed in the cold,
What felled by the light, the darkness has shown.
Above in the sky, the moon has to rise,
As the shadows fall farther into their lies…

A bitter, ugly truth.

Beauty

January 2nd, 2011

It's really not as stunning as it seems,
the outside gleams with light, you see.
But the light is false, cut to the seams,
and you'll find the soul in poisonous sleep.

Whoever said beauty is only skin-deep,
Was obviously a fool.
For if ugly exists, awake or asleep,
Then beauty is more than complexion and jewels.

Tear apart the thrifty skin,
Past the stitches badly sewn in.
Find the soul, dark or light,
It may surprise you, what's inside…

A sickening story to tell…

Alone

Unknown

I feel like the blood is draining out of my hands,
and my mind is slowly shutting down.
The one thing I could never face stands,
and everywhere I hide, I am found.

I want to cry, but no tears are left,
My soul is sick inside me.
I am now painfully adept,
at forgetting those I care to see.

And now, I am alone…

If everyone cared for someone else… Nobody would ever be alone again.

Love.

Unknown

Oh how the words, "How do you do?" Can change a person's day,
and how a friendly greeting takes the sharp-edged pain away.
A simple hug, a word or two, wipes away impending tears,
and trains a person not to hide their sadness and their fears.

Oh how the words, "I love you, Friend," can change a person's life,
And fill a darkened world with light against all strife.
"I'll be here, no matter what," could save a hundred souls,
If only we took our own time to pay a painless toll.

Who else would live? A life to save,
without reason nor a care.
They're truthfully so very brave,
When no one's standing there.

Alone is strong. Together's pain,
to them it's all blended the same.
Without someone else to care,

they've got no faith in broken prayers.

And if we just listened to twenty words,
a soul holds priceless, eternal worth.
Without love to block the pain,
they would bow to oppression, in sickened shame.

Creatures of the unexplored…

Iron Heart

December 28th, 2010

Far under the water, colder than cold,
music is drifting, the order to retain.
In the ice of the oceans and silent untold,
a moving shadow extends his apparent domain...

So muted in silence, the music of life,
the sound of the oceans, heard not by a soul.
Non-ending interlude, above filled with strife,
when the coldness of the waters, have heart's iron hold…

Nonsense, when viewed at a distance… becomes brilliance.

Homework in the Cupboard

Unknown

The stars that craft the orange sky,
homework in the cupboard.
Hanging lonely in the night,
trace through port'n starboard.

Obedience, you must obey.
Anger, you must hate.
Fear, you must shrink of day.
Envy, you must rights debate.

Stars that craft the orange sky,
O variance of that cupboard.
Witness darkness through the light,
and that which marshals of it.

A trick, treason, betrayal… it's all fatal.

Slighted Souls

January 28th, 2011

We've been tricked, we've been stolen,
Our spirits drifting aimlessly.
Bits of our souls are lost, bits are broken,
Left on streets that lived so famously.

More parting words, another dead immortal,
Written in rusted gold and shattered gems.
To a world of flame, another well-earned portal,
A priceless song worth corrupted sense.

A house of solid gold, now heaps of rust,
Molten rainbows adorn the way.
They traded life, they traded trust,
Their one lifetime's fame now scarlet stained.

What is it worth if it fades away?
Riches, fame, all relevant.
Now it's worth your death, your day,
faced with your own lack of benevolence.

Mortal, mortal…

Mortal Fools

February 16th, 2011

Oh alas, this world is full,
Of sufferers and fools.
With their greedy eyes on golden bowls,
Bearing poison wealth and fatal jewels.

Signed their souls onto the endless train,
Alight with fury, rage and hate.
Atop the charred roof lap white-hot flames,
The carriage door is a one-way gate.

Separate now, their bodies cold,
Bearing worthless riches and wealth.
With empty eyes and plain dumb glee,
By soulless hands the gold is felt…

Such an odd concept, words…

Verbosity, the illness

March 26th, 2011

Nothing is naught,
And sickness, illness.
Buying is bought,
Danger is death when treasure is sought…

Forgotten is lost,
And forever, eternity.
A price is a cost,
Freezing is frozen when water is frost…

Brightening is light,
And shadows, darkness.
Later is night,
Blindness is brilliance when a hindrance is sight…

Said in haste and oft regretted…

What Love is a Token?

March 28th, 2011

Such a fantasy of colors,
Such a hypnotic reign.
As such love is growing duller,
Believing limitations are life's bane.

Oh but love, love, what a loosened word,
It flows freely from our lips, like poison.
But love, oh love, what meaning has this term?
What once held life is now a worthless token…

What once held passion is now lost and broken…

Dreamily, sleepily, softly; laden with quiet…

A Realm of Dreams
March 28th, 2011

Slumb'ring in the calmest night,
Haunted by a ghostly presence.
Illuminated by a white-pure light,
Surrounded by a quiet essence.

Slow, like bits of sleepy fog,
Caught upon the breeze.
Lose inside a dream-land bog,
Lost about the foamy seas.

Drifting, on a white-cap wave,
Pages of a story stray.
Maidens fair and knights pure-brave,
See endless night and never-day.

Why have we strayed…?

<u>Soldier Searching</u>

March 30th-31st, 2011

Searching, marching every day,
Wandering all the nights away.
Wishing for a brief respite,
Hoping for the dawn's first light.

Soldier, Soldier,
Who do you seek?
Go faster, go bolder,
Not gentle or meek.

Sickness, illness, fatal so,
Searching for an antidote.
A cure for dead-cold hearts of stone,
Fallen, ill, all alone…

Soldier, Soldier,
Why did you stray?
The path is here for you, sir,
Finally you have found your way…

Fame is irrelevance, even unimportance…

A Synonym of Fame is Fool

April 1st, 2011

Once in fame,
Now broken and alone.
Give credit, or give blame,
To mortals forged of stone.

Remember, or forget,
Believe, or reject.
A way, a path, now lost,
And your soul was the only cost…

Mortal, mortal,
your face is carved in stone.
A likeness to survive,
Through centuries, alone.

Have you requisitioned life?
Fool, believing it to be.
All you've done is hasten strife,
And plant a deadly seed.

Inactivity is a plague…

Restless

April 11th, 2011

Restless, and moving,
We must haste and flee.
From this battle we are losing,
Simply caused by what we've seen.

Sitting still is painful,
Lest I pour out my thoughts.
Life is either sharp or dull,
Due to wars we have fought and lost…

So much more than a simple meaning…

Eloquent, Sir

April 18th, 2011

What else is in eloquence,
Asides a meaning, elegance.
Beyond aforementioned definitions,
Lie unspoken fears, black inhibitions.

I am eloquent, sir,
Swift as the spinning blade's whirr.
Bereft of symbolic failures,
As the white heart grows paler…

But the cost of perfection, supposed, it seems,
Lives by the death of its dark shadow's gleam…
And the opinions of others, all around,
Mean nothing if your own clines down…

An ill-kept obsession is distance…

Longingly Distanced

April 21st, 2011

You make my heart ache,
And I don't know why.
It takes my breath clean away,
To never be part of your life.

I feel like such a fool,
Such a broken-hearted lover.
This fire will never cool,
This book has an empty cover…

My words pour out like a poisonous drink,
They taint the ground with crimson pain.
Beneath the waves my lone thoughts sink,
About the waters with a front of disdain…

Irony is a plague.

Light's End
September 6th, 2011

I am cold.
In a frozen wasteland of time.
I bought my ticket with my soul,
Now this barren wasteland is mine.

No one wanders my cold terrain,
No sunlight plagues my lovely cold.
Sometimes falls a freezing rain,
No colder than my frosty soul.

I think this land is wonderful,
No woods to break my view.
Of course t'is nice, t'was worth my soul,
And only emptiness now ensues.

I watch the skies turn darker still,
This place is so devoid of light.
I took the path with mortal treasure laid,
And so I pay with my wanderings, through eternal night.

Kept in warmth and purity, reigns love for a lovely safety…

A Presence of Safety
April 28th, 2011

It beckons like a trove of gold,
From the heavens, where no foul souls stray.
Untainted by vile mortals' hold,
In peace, here, we will ever stay…

By the hands of God, to Heaven lifted,
Where strife is gone, joy a lovely presence.
Where life is free and dreams are drifting,
And anger passes swiftly in the truth of pure non-chalance…

For eternity, here, we will ever stay, in the cool of the day, never again from God to stray…

An inability to express emotion cultivates fear…

Afraid

May 2nd, 2011

Fear, like a choking grip,
As strong as ever need be.
Sharp as any razor's lip,
Fear for others and their eternal sleep.

What if they won't listen, pray tell?
How will I stop their broken lies?
From dragging them under, to fester in Hell,
While in Heaven, crying for them I abide?

It tears like razor claws at me,
Don't they understand this pain?
Why, oh why, can they not see,
I am unable to help, and so ashamed.

I wish I could show them all,
Every sorrow I have felt, like knives.
But not for myself, what a wasted call,
I pray for hope to those with fear who are dying…

A hopeless story…

Far to Find

May 13th, 2011

It's left me with a hopeless idea,
Replaying endlessly in my shadowed mind.
Just me and you, those blind could see,
You've left me soulsick, hid my heart far to find.

Is it snagged upon a thorn-tree,
All my love crying, bleeding out?
By the time it's found, it will no longer be,
My heart, but an empty shell.

You've condemned my soul to illness,
Such a wraith with poison touch.
You're narcissistic in your stillness,
As I pour out my thoughts like such.

I've told you all, hoping for dawnbreak,
But darkness reigned in your eyes.
On your heart, everything I've staked,
But you've killed it all with your silent lies.

Don't even bother, you coward, you fool.
Too much fear, carelessness, governed your heart.
A shade, a shadow, ever cool,
Why do I bother? Why even start...

Joy is a simple love…

Joy Waking

May 17th, 2011

Like joy, anticipation so,
It walks beside me now.
This moment passes, I wish it slow,
What a pleasant question, why and how…

Don't wonder what brings joy to death,
A simple love can make it so.
Love for anything at all,
Can make fiery hate simmer low.

Of course, my friend, my life is love,
Captured by joy and simple pleasures.
I care for you, as well, my love,
Souls, above all, are the greatest treasures.

A recurring nightmare, we are…

Humanity

May 23rd, 2011

Love, my love, you're far from me,
In the dark, where none can see.
Lost, we're gone, we're broken.
Many ill-meant words are spoken.

How can we hope to survive here,
Where darkness holds reign over all?
Integrity's choked by glares and sneers,
Humanity is sure to fall.

How can light exist in this place,
A small, flickering candle, a flame.
Darkness prowls 'round, fed by hate,
With slith'ring snakes of poison blame.

Like darkness, like evil, turmoil and sin,
Shh, they cry, that's our way! Humanity is all.
Where has all the light gone? Where has beauty been?
Humanity will perish mid-fall…

A wonderful concept is love…

Just Love

June 16th, 2011

Love is so simple in your presence,
Just joy as plain as summer's grass.
You come by light, a lovely essence,
Your intent as clear as shimm'ring glass.

Just love, just you,
Awaiting me in perfect peace.
The clearest skies, seas so blue,
Could never compare to you.

Oh Lord, you love my soul,
Without you I am lost.
You take me up and make me whole,
And to serve you is the only cost.

Just love, just you,
You've come to set me free.
Instruct me, Lord, command me true,
Show me what I'm made to be…

Teach me…

Bidden

June 16th, 2011

What is this beauty surrounding me?
Pure brilliance, this ever gorgeous world.
With golden sun, this land I see,
Untouched by man, still clean, unsoiled.

How could it be, how could it be,
Your haze of peace envelopes me.
Oh Lord, my God, I finally see,
Just what it is I'm meant to be.

Father, will you look here?
See me, Father, I need you.
O everything that I hold dear,
I would sacrifice if you bade me to…

Enchanting colors, hidden beauty…

What Fire

June 16th, 2011

Swirling, leaping flames of red,
Scarlet, broken shards of light.
Wild things, neither alive nor dead,
Dancing shadows dark and bright.

What living fire, curling smoke,
Sleeping or alert, up, not down,
It opens misty eyes when woke,
And flows away, never to be found.

What fire, what tongues of light,
Exceeding attacks of darkest night.
Breaking the curtain of shadows within,
My dreadful tale is now yours to spin…

About the Author

Kelsie Stone, age thirteen, lives in the United States with her family and four dogs. She loves going to church, volunteering for various events and going to the shooting range with her parents. (She prefers her mother's 9 mil. over her father's Glock. It's lighter.) Kelsie loves writing with a passion that far exceeds her age. She was born with an exceptional gift from God for writing, and she lives for Him.

Kelsie fully intends to continue writing and she plans on releasing several more books of the poetry and historical fiction/fiction genres.

Made in the USA
Lexington, KY
05 December 2011